I Love You, Mom

D0770029

My Dear Mom,

I wrote this book because _____

From:

I love you mom because you
made it possible for me to

....

....

"Mother is the heartbeat in every home."

If I could get you anything in the world, it would be

....

....

"No one has loved you like your mom and no one ever will. Her love is the purest of all."

I am very grateful you taught me

....

....

"The highest compliment I could receive is that I've turned into my mother. I can only hope!"

I love you because you can make

....

....

out of nothing.

"Moms are the most beautiful beings in the world."

I love hearing stories about

....

....

"Everything I've learned that's worth knowing, I learned from my mother."

I love you because

you always remember to

....

....

"Nobody loves you like your mom. She's your best friend, your most honest critic, and your biggest fan all rolled into one."

I think you are the best at

....

....

"A mother's love does not set with the sun. It blankets you all through the night."

I love you because you tell

me I am

....

....

There is no role in life
that is more essential
than that of
motherhood

I love you because

you give the best advice when

···

···

"I cherish every moment we spend together, Mom. They are the memories I hold dear to my heart."

Everyone knows that you are

....

....

A mother
understands what a
child does not say

Thank you, mom, for understanding me when

....

....

A mother's arms
are more
comforting than
anyone else's

Lady Diana

It's very funny when you

....

....

"No matter where I go, my mother's voice always brings me home."

I love you because

I know you will never

....

....

The road home is paved with a mother's love. There is always a path back into her arms."

I love you because

you always help me with

....

....

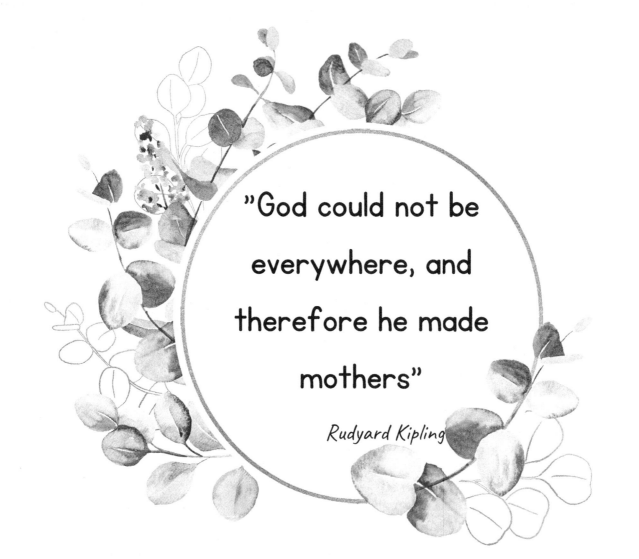

"God could not be everywhere, and therefore he made mothers"

Rudyard Kipling

I love you because

you build me up when

....

....

"To the world, you are a mother, but to your family, you are the world."

You deserve the

....

....

Award

"To a child's ear, 'mother' is magic in any language."

My best memory with you is

....

....

"I can imagine no heroism greater than motherhood."

I love you because you can

....

....

faster than anyone

"I am nothing without my mother. She is the reason for everything I am and all that I will be."

I love you because you can fix

....

....

"My fondest memory of childhood? My mother."

I love you because

you make the yummiest

....

....

"A mother's tears can bring the world to its knees and her joy can cause celebration across the globe."

Together, we make the

absolute best

....

....

TEAM

"Mothers can look through a child's eyes and see tomorrow."

Thank you mom for

encouraging me to

....

....

"Being a mother is learning about strengths you didn't know you had."

If you were a color, you'd be

....

....

"No one works harder than a mother. No one loves harder than a mother. "

I love that you always have the

greatest taste in

....

....

You taught me to see beauty in everything. I see the beauty in you, Mom."

My favorite place where we
have been together is

....

....

"Every day is special when I get to spend it with my mom."

I love that you inspired me to

....

....

"A mother who values her children have children who value her."

I was very proud of you when

....

....

"No one is kinder
or more caring
than a mom."

If you were a holiday, you'd be

....

....

"Moms are the most underappreciated overachievers."

I know you love me because

....

....

"Moms are the biggest blooms in the bouquet of life."

I love that I got from you

....

....

The sound of my mom's voice is the harmony to my melody."

I am really grateful for

....

....

"Wishes are granted in a mother's heart."

The most important
thing I learned from you is

....

....

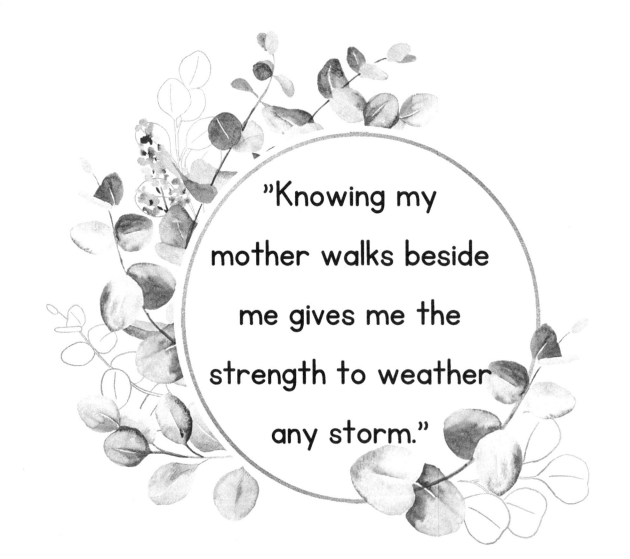

"Knowing my mother walks beside me gives me the strength to weather any storm."

You are the best

mom ever because

....

....

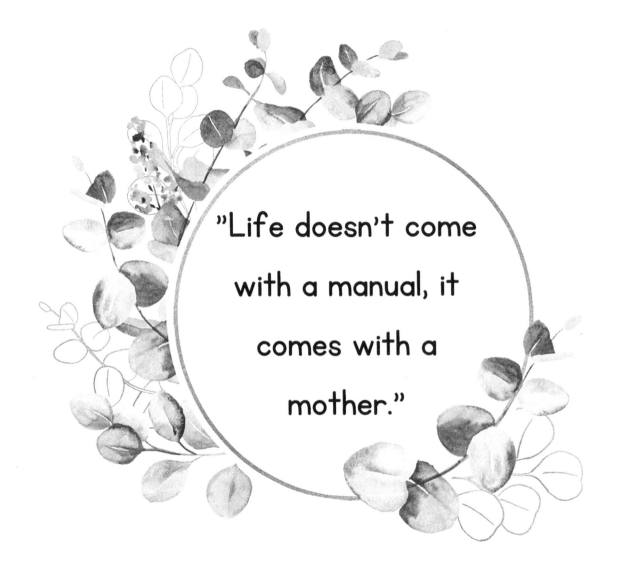

"Life doesn't come with a manual, it comes with a mother."

Want FREEBIES?

Email Us At:

larasvows@gmail.com

Title the email "What I Love About Mom" and let us know that you purchased our book.

_____

THANKS FOR YOUR AMAZING SUPPORT!

>>>>>>>>>>>>>>>>>>>>>>>>>>>>>>>>

For Enquiries and Customer Service
email us at:

larasvows@gmail.com

We don't exist without you. A brief review could help us a lot. Please leave your feedback about this book.

SCAN THE OR CODE BELLOW

>>>>>>>>>>>>>>>>>>>>>>>>>>>>>>>>>

THANKS FOR YOUR AMAZING SUPPORT!

Made in the USA
Coppell, TX
05 May 2022

77461030R00039